THE OSMIROID BOOK OF CALLIGRAPHY

by Christopher Jarman

Published by Osmiroid, Gosport, Hampshire, England.

About the Author

Christopher Jarman

After serving as an officer in the Fleet Air Arm for eight years, Christopher Jarman trained as a teacher at King Alfred's College Winchester and studied calligraphy at Winchester Art School. As a primary school teacher and headmaster he developed a keen interest in the teaching of handwriting and lettering to young children. He became Handwriting Consultant to Osmiroid Pens in 1966.

His books, articles and handwriting scheme based on his Basic Modern Hand are well known and his ideas have been adopted by many local education authorities in the U.K. and abroad.

He is now In-Service Co-ordinator for the Roehampton Institute of Higher Education and an active member of the Society of Scribes and Illuminators.

Acknowledgements

Grateful thanks to the following for permission to use their work:
Barbara Getty – Italic Handwriting
David Graham – Formal Italic Hand and Roman, Gothic, Uncial and Copperplate alphabets

© E. S. Perry Ltd. 1983

Contents

History of Pen Making

About 5,000 years ago the Sumerians, in what is now Iraq, developed writing as wedge shaped, cuneiform letters by pressing the ends of cut reeds into clay. The ancient Egyptians, Greeks and Romans also wrote with reed stalks.

In Roman and Medieval days the largest outer wing feathers of geese or swans were cut for making writing instruments. Roman writers also used a bone stylus on flat wax tablets – hence the word 'style' in writing.

Many attempts were made to make more durable pens than quills, and history attributes the widespread adoption of flexible steel nibs for writing to James Perry, founder of E. S. Perry Ltd., makers of Osmiroid Pens.

150 years ago, in 1830, Letters Patent were granted by King George IV to James Perry:

Ever since the Letters Patent, of which this is an extract, his descendants have been manufacturing steel nibs. Now they are gold plated for smoother writing and provided in Osmiroid fountain pens, through the English company E. S. Perry Limited which manufactures them.

A.D. 1830 . . . . Nº 5933.

"An Improvement or Improvements in or on Pens;"

PERRY'S SPECIFICATION.

TO ALL TO WHOM THESE PRESENTS SHALL COME, I, James Perry, of Red Lion Square, Holborn, in the County of Middlesex, Bookseller and Stationer, send greeting.

WHEREAS His late most Excellent Majesty King George the Fourth, did by His Letters Patent under the Great Seal of Great Britain, bearing date at Westminster, the Twenty-fourth day of April, in the eleventh year of His reign, give and grant unto me, the said James Perry, His special licence, that I, the said James Perry, my executors, administrators, and assigns.

Pen Nibs designed 150 years ago by James Perry

This drawing accompanies the Letters Patent granted by George IV which marked the beginning of the Osmiroid tradition.

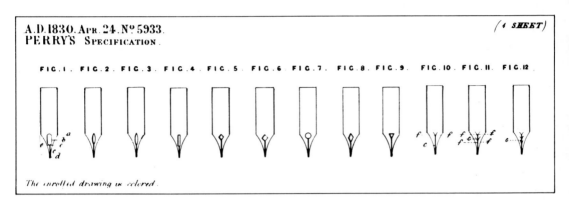

A.D. 1830. Apr. 24. Nº 5933.
PERRYS Specification.

(1 SHEET)

FIG. 1.   FIG. 2.   FIG. 3.   FIG. 4.   FIG. 5.   FIG. 6.   FIG. 7.   FIG. 8.   FIG. 9.   FIG. 10.   FIG. 11.   FIG. 12.

The enrolled drawing is colored.

How to use this book

In this book you will find many different calligraphic alphabets. The most basic ones such as Roman and Gothic are shown with arrows to indicate which way you should move your broad nib in order to construct each letter. To begin with, always choose a nib width which is the same as the one used in the example you are copying. The reason is that the proportions of black ink area and white space in a letter are very important. Practise by copying letters the same size as the model too. Every size of lettering has its exact width of nib and that is what will help your letters to look right. You will notice on all the early pages, these marks

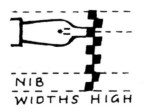

NIB
WIDTHS HIGH

These are to indicate the measure of the height of letters in nib widths.

Later in the book there are some larger letters written with pens cut from bamboo stalks. Naturally as the pen widths are much wider the letter heights are greater.

How to get started

The art of beautiful writing, known as Calligraphy, is an ideal leisure pursuit for anyone to enjoy.

With the help of this book and your pens, you can soon develop your very own style of Calligraphy – a style as personal to you as your own signature. Everything you write can become eyecatching – greeting cards, personalised stationery, invitations, letters, posters, labels, handwritten poems, family trees and beautiful handwriting of every kind.

Use a black fountain pen ink. Do not use waterproof India Ink as it looks shiny and also gums up your nibs – unless you have a fountain pen specially designed to work with India Ink.

All you need in addition to your pens and ink is a smooth non-absorbent writing or drawing paper, whose surface allows you to make the letters easily and rhythmically. Pad your writing surface with several sheets of blotting paper or cartridge paper to give a soft padded writing surface.

You may wish to rule feint lines or to sketch the layout of the page before writing it in ink. A sharp H or HB pencil, a soft eraser, a set square and a rule would then become useful.

You will need to relax and concentrate all your attention on learning and understanding the letter shapes.

Sit in a comfortable position at a table with reasonable light. Before beginning to write you should practise holding the pen and controlling it correctly. The pen must be held between the thumb and forefinger and should rest on the middle finger. It should be held consistently at an angle of 30 degrees or 45 degrees to the writing line as indicated for each style.

The whole hand should be moved to manipulate the pen, not just the thumb and forefinger. If you find your fingers becoming cramped, relax the grip on your pen.

The best seated position for writing is with feet flat on the floor, back fairly straight. The paper should be set straight and immediately in front of you on the writing surface.

Start by putting the broadest nib into your pen and practise the following four exercises.

Consistency is an important feature of Calligraphy and rhythmic practise of these exercises before each writing session will help you to control your writing.

The shapes of letters have evolved according to ease and speed of writing and many of the basic strokes needed for lettering are incorporated in these strokes.

Work on one alphabet at a time – there are many presented in this booklet for you to learn. Once you have mastered the Roman alphabet, you will find it much easier to learn the others.

Roman Hand –

based on English 10th Century forms.

The pointed serif ◢ is done like this: ◢

Roman Capital Letters

This Roman alphabet is based upon Edward Johnston's Foundational Hand. It is sometimes called 10th Century Winchester. The small letters or minuscules are also known as English Carolingian as their rounded form was developed in England during the reign of the Emperor Charlemagne. Johnston actually based his own Foundational Hand upon writing in the Ramsey Psalter. This was a book of psalms written by a scribe in Huntingdonshire in the 10th century. It is called Foundational because if it is practised and mastered first, then scribes today believe that most other styles will be achieved more easily later.

The Formal Italic Style

The Fine Italian hand was developed early in the sixteenth century in Italy. A scholar from Florence, Niccolo de Niccoli developed a fast joined style by linking the Carolingian minuscules and using the hand for informal correspondence, not only for books. One of Pope Eugenius' chief scribes in The Vatican in 1522 took Niccoli's style as a model and developed a fast style based on oval shapes. This scribe was Ludovico degli Arrighi. His copybook cut from wood blocks and known as the Operina is considered the first writing book or copybook.

Today apart from italic handwriting which is the informal style, formal italic is also a very popular form of lettering. It is very suitable for lively work such as posters, book jackets, envelopes and invitation cards, greetings etc. Menus and programmes also look well in italic. We only call it 'Formal' to distinguish it from handwriting. Actually italic lends itself to spirited and less serious occasions.

Formal Italic Hand

The Chancery hand, used by scribes in the Papal business offices during the 16th Century, became the basis for a wide variety of beautiful Italic written forms and type faces.

Swash Capitals
may be made by
extending the strokes.

ABCDEFGHIJKLM
NOPQRSTUVWXYZ

Gothic or Black Letter

Many amateur scribes begin as children copying out Gothic or Olde English as it is sometimes called. It has an antique air of respectability about it and was used by the Victorians and Edwardians to give authority to memorials, many church notices and legal documents.

This air of authority still remains today in its use by certain newspapers for their name headings. To the professional scribe Black Letter is the term used to describe hundreds of different examples of this style. No particular one is correct and just one of many is shown here. It is called black letter because the white spaces are close together more than other styles. It began around the 12th Century, some say due to inflation and the price of vellum being so high that scribes began compressing more words per page! The main thing to remember is that the vertical lines should be evenly spaced like a picket fence. The aim with this style is more to be decorative than legible. Lloyd Reynolds, the American calligrapher and teacher called it the 'christmas alphabet' as we usually only read it at that season.

Gothic or Black Letter

To achieve an economy of space, Medieval letters became increasingly compressed, creating a strong visual texture.

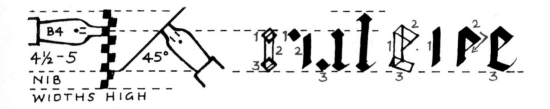

aabcdefghhijklm

nopqrzsstuvvw

wxyz

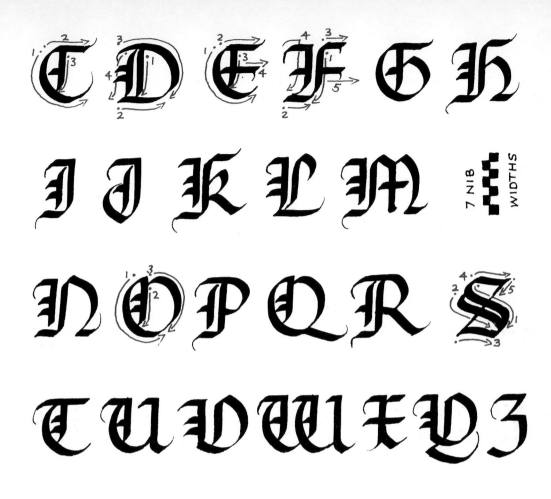

Uncial Letters

Uncials are really developed from Roman capitals. Between the 5th and the 9th Century these rounded and slightly more relaxed forms of capitals became faster to write. The minuscules of the English Carolingian style were gradually created from the uncial and half uncial forms. Uncials are characteristic of much early christian writing. The forms are generous and round. The pen is either held vertically so that the widest stroke is upright, or a right oblique nib is used, allowing the right handed writer to relax a little. There are many many forms of uncial, the example shown by David Graham, is based upon 6th Century examples.

Uncial Hand

This round 6th Century pen form omits the serifs of the Roman Capital letters, establishes new 'small letter' forms, based on hand writing movements.

ɛᖴᎶ𝗁𝗂𝗃𝗄ʟᴍ

ᴎᴏᴘᴏ̨ɋʀѕᴛ

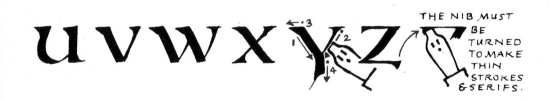

Copperplate

Originally engraved on copper plates for intaglio printing, the forms became so popular that pointed quills and later flexible nibs were devised to permit the use of pressure in writing to simulate the swelling thick thin line, which became so characteristic of 19th Century handwriting.

Italic Handwriting

HOW TO SIT
For best results, sit with your feet resting flat
on the floor and your forearms resting
on a table or desk.
Try not to slump!

Writing

PAPER POSITION
If righthanded, slant your paper slightly to the
left – reverse if lefthanded. Find a convenient area in
which to write – then each time you write a few words,
shift the paper with your non-writing hand. A
slanted surface will add to your writing enjoyment.

PEN HOLD
Hold pen comfortably between your thumb
and forefinger resting it on the middle finger.
The shaft should rest near the large knuckle. Try
not to pinch the pen – a comfortable hold
will result in better handwriting.

Reminders

PEN ANGLE

The edge of the nib should lie at an angle
of 45° to the writing line in order to allow the pen
to form the correct thicks and thins as you write.

THIS ITALIC ALPHABET is derived from the beautiful
16th century Roman hand. It is written with a chisel edged
nib held at a CONSTANT 45° angle to the writing line.

By holding the
pen in this
manner, you
are assured
of the proper

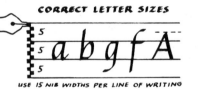

CORRECT LETTER SIZES

USE 15 NIB WIDTHS PER LINE OF WRITING

"thicks" \\\ and "thins" /// that add to the beauty and
character of the letters. HOLD the pen shaft near the large
knuckle to ensure that the entire nib edge contacts the paper.

TRY THESE BASIC STROKES

USE MEDIUM OR LARGER NIB:

*Try NOT to pinch your pen! Remember, this is HANDWRITING not finger
writing.*

THE LOWER CASE ALPHABET *is shown below in family groups for easier mastery. Trace the letters of one group to get the feel — then write them. Be patient with yourself!*

KEEP NIB EDGE AT 45° · SLOPE LETTERS ABOUT 5° TO THE RIGHT

lihnrmu · k · oce

BASIC FAMILY SHAPE   OMIT BEGINNING SERIF ON *i · u · y* WHEN USING JOINS

adgq · bp · tfsj · vwxyz

WORDS TO WRITE — *hill rim hum run · kin · choice · adage quick gage · probe brought · fast jump · vex wise yes zest · practice!*

REMEMBER THESE FOUR HINTS —
1 *no joins before ascenders · b f h k l*
2 *no joins after descenders · f g j p q y*
3 *no joins from capitals*
4 *avoid ALL loops e.g., k, j*

for fluency

Write these words for practice

os amaryllis · begonia · crocus · dogwood
edelweiss · flax · geranium · huckleberry · ivy · jasmine

USE THE PLAIN CAPITALS *for* ALL *occasions.*
They are based on the classical ROMAN *letter*

CAPITAL
LETTERS

forms — but slant these
letters slightly to the
right.   Use the plain
capitals for captions,
titles, addresses — when-
ever you'd like emphasis.

Write capital letters at 7 or 8 nib widths.

(NOTE: THE CAPS ARE NOT JOINED TO LOWERCASE LETTERS)

ABCDEFGHIJKLMN
OPQRSTUVWXY&Z

Basic Modern Hand

In recent years there has been an upsurge of interest in the teaching of handwriting in schools. The infant schools in particular have suffered in the past through teaching a print script which was based upon 10th Century lettering. It is now realised that children must be taught a basic hand with movements which need not change once they have been learnt. Osmiroid has been instrumental in encouraging the Basic Modern Hand designed by Christopher Jarman specifically for use in modern primary and secondary schools. It is based upon the Italic oval structure for speed and economy, but may be written with any modern writing instrument as well as a chisel edged pen later on.

It is taught in three stages and based upon eight fundamental patterns.

Pattern	*Value of Pattern*
mmmm	r n m h p b k
ccccc	c o a d g q e
uuuuuu	i u y l t
wwwwww	v w x
uuuuuu	i u y l t a d
mmmmm	r n p m h
oooooooo	c o oo oa og od
ililililil	i l u m h

Basic Modern Hand

Stage One

a b c d e f g h i j k l m n
o p q r s t u v w x y z

Stage Two, hooks added prior to joining

a b c d e f g h i j k l m n
o p q r s t u v w x y z

Stage Three, joined where appropriate only

abcdefghijklmn
opqrstuvwxyz

The Capital Letters

A B C D E F G H I J K L M N
O P Q R S T U V W X Y Z

Left-Handers and Calligraphy

There are two kinds of nibs made for left-handers. The most common is the left oblique or 'cropped' nib which is made in all of the lettering sizes. Because of the angle, the width of the line drawn by a 'cropped' nib is slightly larger than its normal equivalent nib.

In the italic handwriting range the cranked nib is also made.

Left oblique nib

Cranked nib

Left handers will find it easier to write if they

1. Tilt the paper to the right

2. Use a slightly higher chair or lower table than normal.

Roll the pen between the fingers until it is in a position easily to make this pattern.

Shadow Calligraphy

Different Types of Nib

There are an enormous number of nibs now made commercially both for fountain pens and for dipping direct into ink. You must experiment with them all for various effects. Remember that it is not the nib which will improve your calligraphy, it is your calligraphy that will control the nib! There are specialist nibs of all kinds from shorthand, to sketch and music nibs. It is possible to achieve many effects by trying out these various types. You should also try making your own nibs from matchbox wood, bamboo and quills of varying sizes.

Recently, Osmiroid have manufactured a range of broad fountain pen nibs which write with a double line. They are called Shadow nibs. Some useful effects may be obtained using them, but be careful not to overdo it. They are probably most suitable for headings, titles, patterns, nameplates, etc. but usually not for long passages of writing.

To get the feel of using shadow nibs try these patterns. Remember: both tips of the shadow nib must touch the paper at the same time.

Here are some examples of the effects that can be achieved with lettering using shadow nib units.

5 nib widths

abcdefgh
ijklmnopq
rstuvwxyz
abcdefg

Some flourishes

and some very distinctive nameplates.

FIONA

David Anne

Margaret

More examples using a broad nib.

Making Your Own Pens

As well as using metal nibs for ease and reliability, it is interesting to make pens from natural materials. Goose, swan and turkey wing feathers are suitable for quills. For very large lettering, bamboo and other hollow stalked wood may be used. The principles of cutting such pens are similar for both quill and bamboo. Feathers should be large and well dried in an airing cupboard or oven; bamboo is easiest cut when it is green. First cuts are best made with a fine-toothed saw when making a bamboo pen.

Make a long angled cut of the quill or bamboo first.

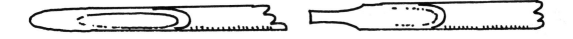

Then pare the sides evenly to make the width of nib desired.

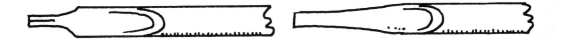

Turn the pen face down and chop across to make a straight end. With a quill you will need to cut a slit:

but this is not necessary with a bamboo or reed pen, as being naturally fibrous they will retain and release ink in their capilliary structure. Various kinds of reservoirs may be fitted and are described in Edward Johnston's 'Writing, Illuminating and Lettering'. Also there is a very informative article by Ewan Clayton in 'The Scribe' SSI Journal Summer 1983.

It is easy to make your own bamboo pens and very cheap. Also you are able to control entirely what size and type of nib you have. In general bamboos are better for large writing on posters etc.

Calligraphic Drawings

Practising beautiful lettering and writing is so absorbing and time consuming that many students become fixed upon the notion of 'getting it right'. This is a good attitude up to a point but can result in some people taking calligraphy almost too seriously and making a series of very dull and imitative exercises out of it.

With constant practice, the control of a pen can become easier and more free. Using occasional faint pencil guide sketches, it is possible to work out very calligraphic images. The flourishes and whirls of the 18th Century copper engravers provide some exciting starting points for ideas.

If you can draw at all, then try some drawings deliberately utilising the advantages of the chisel edged pen. Look at some of the border illustrations in some medieval books. Try decorating your own capital letters and above all try using COLOUR.

Some basic strokes with broad pens.

Strokes with a double-line pen nib.

Very wide pens may be made of metal or felt tipped. They have exciting possibilities.

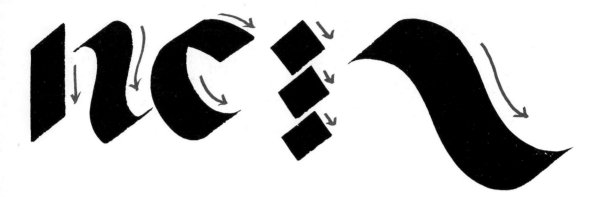

Wide pens may also be cut from reeds or green bamboo canes.

The same patterns done in very large sizes look different from those made with a small nib –

Calligraphic drawing has a very ancient history. Man has always felt a mystical impulse to make shapes out of words and words out of shapes. Poems in particular lend themselves to being visually shaped and the modern 'poetry concrete' is the contemporary expression of such creativity. In the 3rd Century B.C. in Greece shaped writing was called technopaegnia.

Japanese and Chinese calligraphers have always thought of the content and form of poems and other writings as one. In the Muslim world the stern forbidding of any graven or painted image of God meant that decorative calligraphy as an abstract art was developed to a very high degree. A Persian calligrapher, Mullah Mir Ali, once said 'My pen works miracles and rightly enough is the form of my words proud of its superiority over its meaning'. In Tibet people will not destroy any paper upon which a word is written because to them the word and the object are one and so is the name of a thing.

Drawings and flourishes based on those of Tagliente, a 16th Century scribe. Copy AND invent!

Have fun with

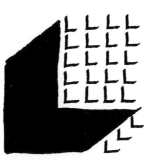

It is a pleasant and amusing exercise for the calligrapher to portray a written word made of letters also as an illustration of the object.

A calligraphic drawing can be called a calligram and on the next page there are some examples. More can be found in medieval manuscripts. A useful book for further study is 'Word as Image' by Berjouhi Bowler published by Studio Vista.

38

A bold scribble is the best way to give
yourself ideas. This became a bird's wing.

The Uses of Calligraphy

Once you have mastered one or two basic alphabets and have experimented with some calligraphic drawings and different layouts, try some creative uses of your new skill.

Layouts

Do not always stick to the conventional upright sheet of paper or card. Nor need you only write on white or cream paper. Try white designers colour on black or dark blue paper.

Some suggested layouts.

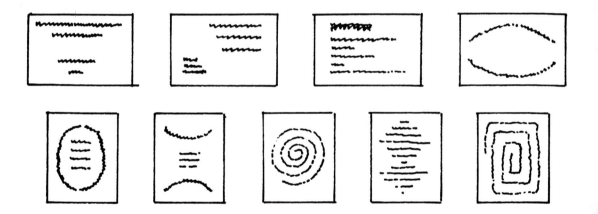

Uses for Your Skill

Announcements. Banners. Business Cards. Bookplates. Brochures. Catalogues. Certificates. Condolences. Commendations. Christmas Cards. Congratulations. Diplomas. Family Trees. Envelopes. Guest Places. Menus. Inscriptions. Invitations. Letterheads. Memorials. Mottos. Logos. Name tags. Poems. Posters. Scrolls. Testimonials. Signs. Speeches. Show cards. Title pages. etc. etc.

Envelopes

Graphologists say that to decorate an envelope or to write names and addresses with excessive flourish is a sure sign that the writer wishes to draw attention to himself. I think it is hard to disagree with this. My own version of this thought would be 'If you've got it, flaunt it'! The recipients of unusually flourished envelopes are invariably delighted at the implied compliment, for however skilled a calligrapher may be, designing and executing an interesting name and address takes time.

This is one of the few times in calligraphy when waterproof ink may be a good idea, as envelopes are subject to handling and weather. Another useful tip is to wax over the finished address with the side of a white wax candle.

The discipline of designing an envelope is a very useful one and it is best to stick to not more than two styles of lettering. Two or three colours can be used with care. Any colour of envelope is suitable provided it is fairly light. Chinese white is quite pleasant on a dark envelope but has a tendency to smudge. A little gum arabic in the paint mix helps.

If very large nibs are to be used, perhaps a bamboo pen, then make sure you have a large envelope. All lettering needs a space around it. Do not choose lettering that is too bizarre or 'gothic' in character as the address may not be legible and the whole point of the exercise becomes lost!

Practice makes perfect and playing about with envelope shape and letter design will help to give you confidence. The shadow nibs are particularly suited to envelopes.

Reference: Lettering and Decorating Envelopes by Diana Hutchinson.
Calligraphy Ideas Exchange – Vol. One No. 2. 1983.

Top right: A straightforward, plain but attractive envelope.

Bottom right: More flowery style, artistic but still traditional.

Christopher Jarman Esq:
Osmiroid Works
Gosport
Hants

Christopher Jarman, Esq.;
The School House,
Sibford Gower,
BANBURY
Oxford

Royal College of Art   Kensington Gore London SW7

DUBAY
1805 N.W. 34th Avenue
Portland, Oregon 97210

Opuntia basilaris

USA 20c

Beavertail Cactus USA 20c

Ferocactus wislizenii

Barrel Cactus

Christopher
WHITELANDS COLLEGE
West Hill
Jarman
London SW15 35N
ENGLAND

USAirmail

PORTLAND
R SEP
1978

CHRIS

JARMAN !
22 Westland Way
Woodstock
OXFORD
England

Top left: More adventurous, using two pens and a thoughtful layout of address.

Bottom left: A more dramatic use of colour, contrasting pen sizes and design.

Below: One of the very many beautiful envelopes which are received at Perry's frequently.

Examples of Calligraphy for the Amateur

Having written to one's friends in an informal italic style and designed some eye catching envelopes, it is worth trying your hand at some other enterprises. First, try to sign on at a recognised calligraphy course. These are held all over the country in evening classes and weekend courses. 'Recognised' means run by a member of the Society of Scribes and Illuminators – the S.S.I. – if in the U.K. In the U.S.A. there are a number of similarly recognised bodies allied to the S.S.I. Do not merely copy out alphabets. Try to risk writing out a poem or a favourite proverb or saying and give to a friend. People practise all their lives and never feel that they are good enough. This can be very destructful and inhibiting. Have a go. Try making up new designs and using colours.

The following pages show some examples of how amateur scribes have used their pens to write out pieces of prose, invent logos, record useful phrases or greetings.

How to draw yourself an

for breakfast

To choose or construct
beautiful forms
requires good taste,
and that in its turn
requires cultivation,
which comes from the
observation of beautiful
forms. Those who are not
accustomed to seeing
beautiful things are, in
consequence, often
uncertain whether they
think a thing beautiful or
not. Some – perhaps all
of us – have an intuition
for what is beautiful; but
most of us have to achieve
beauty by taking pains.

From 'Writing Lettering and Illuminating'

by Edward Johnston.

Always look ahead there are no regrets in that direction

Wilbur Smith

The Chaos
About thee
is but the
Confusion
within
Thee

Design for a Christmas card

Some of the early Semitic names for letters of the alphabet.

Ox Aleph *house* Beth

camel Gimel *door* Daleth

He Waw *hook*

weapon Zayin Heth

Teth Yod *hand*

palm Kaph Lamed *rod*

Mem Nun *fish*

fish Samekh

The
delicate little down
strokes curved with an
edged pen lend them-
selves beautifully to
the construction of
plants & seed
pods.

In Conclusion

Like all crafts such as pottery, weaving or carving etc., calligraphy is very difficult to master. The more you learn, the more you realise there is to learn. The professional never ceases to strive for greater mastery. Anyone who chooses to earn a living at a craft knows of its subtleties and of the dangers of exploiting easily learnt tricks, and results based upon mere slickness.

For the enthusiastic amateur, the serious dedication of the skilled professional is often so daunting that one is discouraged from trying at all. Or perhaps the amateur does try by fearfully imitating other people's alphabets and constantly repeating letters over and over again, unable to strike out and enjoy the almost sensual experience of pen and ink.

This book has been aimed at those who need encouragement to express themselves, within the discipline of the craft, but without the haunting anxiety that they may have somehow got it wrong. For the professional scribe there will be many self-imposed rules, much knowledge of letter forms, their historical development and so on. But for the amateur, or the hobbyist, action and enjoyment is more important. Perhaps eventually through playing about with pens, the reader may come to appreciate even more the dedication of those calligraphers who have spent years in studying the craft. Who knows, even though in a busy life you may never get the time to practise, you may become a patron or a collector of fine calligraphy, and in doing so help to keep alive and growing one of the oldest and finest arts, the art of beautiful writing.

OSMIROID produce the world's largest range of fountain pen nibs for fine writing, calligraphy, drawing and music writing.

Right Hand

Rola Extra-fine.

Rola fine soft

Rola Fine Hard

Rola medium soft.

Rola medium hard.

Rola broad soft.

R.M. Tipped Medium

Sketch

Copperplate

B2

B3

B4

B5

B6

SH4

SH5

SH6

italic extra fine straight

italic fine straight

*italic fine
inter medium*

*italic
medium straight*

*italic broad
straight*

Left Hand

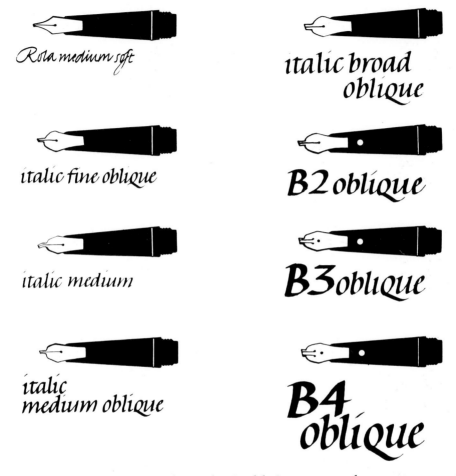

Rola medium soft

italic fine oblique

italic medium

*italic
medium oblique*

*italic broad
oblique*

B2 oblique

B3 oblique

*B4
oblique*

Many of the nibs illustrated are obtainable in a range of pen sets manufactured by Osmiroid for calligraphy, italic writing, drawing and sketching.

The above nibs are for use only with high-quality fountain-pen ink or calligraphers' ink. For those who prefer to use water-proof ink, OSMIROID also offers a growing range of India ink nibs, as well as a sketch pen and a music composition pen.

This book has been sponsored by E.S. Perry Ltd. manufacturers of OSMIROID specialist fountain-pens and nibs for calligraphy and drawing. For more information, see your nearest art materials shop or pen dealer, or write

in the U.S., to: Hunt Manufacturing Company,
1405 Locust Street,
Philadelphia, PA 19102

in the U.K., to: E.S. Perry Ltd.,
Gosport, Hampshire PO13 0AL,
England.

NOTES

NOTES

NOTES

NOTES

Cover by David Williams.
Design by IDA, 2 Serjeants' Inn, London EC4Y 1LU.
Printed by Eyre & Spottiswoode Ltd., Grosvenor Press, Portsmouth, England.